Reason, Induction, and Causation
in Hume's Philosophy

Don Garrett and Peter Millican

The Institute for Advanced Studies in the Humanities
The University of Edinburgh
2011

Garrett, Don and Millican, Peter
Reason, Induction, and Causation in Hume's Philosophy

This series of occasional papers is published by

The Institute for Advanced Studies in the Humanities
The University of Edinburgh
2 Hope Park Square
Edinburgh EH8 9NW

Published July 2011
Copyright © Don Garrett and Peter Millican 2011

All rights reserved. No part of this publication may be reproduced, stored, or transmitted in any form without the written permissions of the authors.

ISSN 2041-8817
ISBN 978-0-9568610-3-0
IASH Occasional Papers, 19

About the Authors

DON GARRETT is Professor and Chair of the Department of Philosophy at New York University. He has taught previously at Harvard University, the University of Utah, and the University of North Carolina at Chapel Hill, where he was Kenan Distinguished Professor for Teaching Excellence. He is the author of *Cognition and Commitment in Hume's Philosophy* (Oxford University Press, 1997) and the forthcoming *Hume* (Routledge). In addition, he is the editor of *The Cambridge Companion to Spinoza* and has served as editor of *Hume Studies* and as North American editor of the *Archiv für Geschichte der Philosophie*. He was recently elected to the American Academy of Arts and Sciences. He is currently Carnegie Centenary Professor at the University of Edinburgh.

PETER MILLICAN is Reader in Early Modern Philosophy at the University of Oxford, and Gilbert Ryle Fellow in Philosophy at Hertford College, Oxford. He is also Illumni David Hume Fellow at the Institute for Advanced Studies in the Humanities, University of Edinburgh, and Honorary Visiting Professor at the University of York. From 2005 until 2010, he was Co-Editor of *Hume Studies*. Prior to his appointment at Oxford, he taught for 20 years at the University of Leeds, where he was Senior Lecturer in Philosophy and Computing, and Founder Director of the Leeds Electronic Text Centre. He recently unveiled a new electronic edition of Hume's *Dialogues* (both text and original manuscript) hosted at www.davidhume.org – the major Hume resource on the web – which he runs together with Amyas Merivale, who works at the Leeds Etext Centre. Peter's philosophical interests and publications cover a wide range but with a particular focus on David Hume and related topics in epistemology, philosophy of religion, and ethics.

Susan Manning: Welcome everybody to the Institute for Advanced Studies. Thank you all for packing in like sardines – I think it's an indication of the interest and enthusiasm people have for what promises to be an intimate [laughter] and also a very feisty dialogue, the final one of our series *Dialogues with Hume*, commemorating the three hundredth anniversary of the birth of David Hume this year. We couldn't have two more eminent or more adversarial ... [laughter] ... Humeans than our two speakers today. We're extremely lucky to be able to bring together in one room for your entertainment and education this afternoon Professor Don Garrett and Dr Peter Millican. I would just like to introduce them very briefly, so that we can have maximum time for hearing them in dialogue. Don Garrett is currently here as Carnegie Centenary Professor at the Institute, and we are very grateful to the Carnegie Trust for the Universities of Scotland for making his visit to Edinburgh possible. He's doing a lot of duty for us and for Scottish universities as a whole while he's here as Carnegie Professor. In other life, he is Professor and Chair for the Department of Philosophy at New York University. He has taught previously at Harvard, the University of Utah, and the University of North Carolina at Chapel Hill where he was Kenan Distinguished Professor for Teaching Excellence; so he teaches as well as philosophizes. He is best known in the philosophical and Humean community for his *Cognition and Commitment in Hume's Philosophy*, which came out in 1997 and he has a forthcoming book on Hume, which is going to be a very important addition to the literature. As well as this, he's editor of the *Cambridge Companion to Spinoza* and he was recently elected to the American Academy of Arts and Sciences.

Then to Don's left, we have Dr Peter Millican who is Reader in Early Modern Philosophy at the University of Oxford and Gilbert Ryle Fellow in Philosophy at Hertford College, Oxford. We've also been extremely fortunate to have Peter with us over the last year on and off at the Institute, and he has also done sterling duty for the University and for the Edinburgh community at large – some of you may have attended his wonderful lecture for the Royal Society last month. That was a terrific occasion. We've also had several opportunities to hear him talk about different aspects of Hume while he's been here. Peter is with us courtesy of the Ilumni David Hume Fellowship, which was very generously offered to us by an anonymous group in Edinburgh, and we hope that it will be an avatar of a longer-term David Hume Tercentenary Fellowship, which we are trying to raise money for at the moment because it seems that Edinburgh, above all, should be the home of a regular series of eminent Humeans, such as we've been privileged to host in the past two years. Further information about that appeal is available after the session if you should like to have it. But let me just tell you more about Peter's work. He is one of the most eminent British Humeans. He has been Co-Editor of *Hume Studies* and indeed is the only Co-Editor of the Hume journal to come from outside North America. He is now, as I said, teaching at Oxford, but before his Oxford time he taught for twenty years at the University of Leeds, where he was Senior Lecturer in Computing and Philosophy and Founder Director of the Leeds Electronic Text Centre. Peter has been instrumental in establishing a new and very innovative degree in Computer Science and Philosophy at Oxford. And knowing something about the Oxbridge system as I do, I can say that is no small achievement, bringing in something new! However, I don't want to take any more of our time right now because we want to hear Peter and Don. So I will leave you to it: 'Reason, Induction, and Causation in Hume's Philosophy'.

Peter Millican: We'll divide this session into two parts, and begin with induction and reason, which we're putting together as a single topic; then we'll go on to causation. I'm going to start by introducing induction and reason, then I'll hand over to Don to say his piece, and then I'll say mine. We'll have some discussion before we move on, with roles reversed for causation.

One of Hume's most original, important and famous arguments concerns the drawing of inferences to 'matters of fact' that we have not (yet) observed. Suppose, for example, that I see one billiard ball rolling fast towards another; I infer that they will collide and that the second ball will then move. Why? According to Hume, any such inference has to be based on experience and involves extrapolating from past to future, or from observed to unobserved. This sort of inference – we call it inductive inference these days, but Hume called it 'probable reasoning' or 'reasoning concerning matter of fact' – takes for granted, or presupposes, according to Hume, a principle of extrapolation: that the behaviour of unobserved things will resemble that of observed things. So we're supposing that things will go on the way they have. This is commonly called Hume's 'Uniformity Principle'.

Hume's argument considers, and in turn rejects, various ways of trying to establish this Uniformity Principle. Having rejected them all, he concludes in the *Treatise* that inductive inferences 'are not determin'd by reason' [Hume 1739-40 (henceforth '*Treatise*'), 1.3.6.12] or in the *Enquiry* that 'our conclusions from [experience] are *not* founded on reasoning, or any process of the understanding' [Hume 1748 (henceforth '*Enquiry*'), 4.15]. Traditionally, this has been interpreted as a radically sceptical result, implying that induction falls outside the domain of reason, thus making it non-rational, perhaps even irrational. But this would seem to imply that inductive inference from experience is no better than soothsaying. If you want to know about the future, why use induction rather than any other method? There are all sorts of superstitious methods for telling the future, and it sounds like induction is no better than them if it's not part of reason. But such scepticism is very hard to square with a great deal of what Hume wrote, because he famously extolled the virtues of introducing the experimental method of reasoning into 'the science of man', and forthrightly condemned superstition. Interpreters such as Antony Flew [1961] and David Stove [1973] accused Hume of being embarrassingly inconsistent, but Hume's defenders soon rallied to his defence against this implausibly crude accusation.

When Don and I came to this problem, twenty years or so ago, the orthodox solution to Hume's apparent inconsistency was to see him as operating with two different notions of 'reason', a strict rationalistic notion within the famous argument, and a looser, naturalistic sense elsewhere. So when Hume says induction isn't founded on reason or determined by reason, he's using the word 'reason' in a very narrow sense that demands *total certainty*. Then the point of the argument could be seen as precisely to *reject* this rationalistic notion, by showing its complete impotence outside the narrow realm of deductive reasoning, mathematics and so forth: if reason, so conceived, was unable even to tell us that a billiard ball would move when hit, then this was clearly a hopelessly inadequate conception of human reason. But Hume himself had a quite different and far less extreme notion of human reason; at least that was the story. This style of interpretation, first proposed in 1975 by Tom Beauchamp and Thomas Mappes, quickly became dominant, being presented with slight variations in influential publications by at least half a dozen authors. But both Don and I – coming to the problem in the late 1980s, quite independently – came up with very similar objections to it, which seemed to us to refute it outright. We came to know each other's work when my long 1995 paper and Don's 1997 book were both going through their respective presses. That's really what got us going, arguing about these things. I think it is fair to say that the particular style of interpretation we were both attacking was pretty much killed stone dead one way or another; at least, I don't think anyone has defended it since, or made any effort to respond to our objections.

Although Don and I were very much agreed about the objections to be made to these previous interpretations, we had very different solutions of our own. The problem was to make sense of how Hume could on the one hand be saying that induction was not determined by reason, but on the other hand, be a great supporter of induction. Don's approach, inspired mainly by Hume's argument in the *Treatise*, took Humean reason to be, quite unambiguously, the faculty of inference, argument, rather than of rationality in general. Thus interpreted, the conclusion of the famous argument – that induction is not 'determin'd by reason' – says not that induction is non-rational, but only that our inductive inferences are not themselves produced by any mediating inference. That was Don's line. My own line, inspired more by Hume's argument in the *Enquiry*, took reason in the famous argument to be a Lockean notion, based on the idea of *perception of truth*, and incorporating not only inference but also self-evidence (what Locke and Hume call 'intuition'), and I took that to be part of reason even though it's not argumentative or inferential in any mediated, stepwise sense. And also, reason consults the deliverances of the senses. But unlike Don, I retained the orthodox view that Hume was operating with more than one notion of reason, and that the famous argument's role was to reject the previously established notion in favour of a broader Humean conception.

Very soon after Don's book appeared, he and I debated all this at the Monterey Hume Conference of 1997 and in subsequent *Hume Studies* publications in 1998. In retrospect, I still find a lot of valuable points made in that discussion, but I think it is fair to say that for both of us, attack was more successful than defence! After researching in detail the 'faculty' language of Hume and his contemporaries, I became convinced two years ago that Don had been right all along in his lonely insistence (because he was standing out against pretty much everybody else) that the notion of reason within the famous argument is Hume's own, rather than a rival conception being set up for refutation. If you remember, the first paper I gave here at IASH when I came last year was on exactly this topic: Hume's faculties. But I am also more than ever convinced that I was right to see reason as significantly broader than just a faculty of inference. Today Don and I have the opportunity to review where we stand on the issue, fourteen years after our Monterey meeting, with – I believe – far more now in common than dividing us. From my own point of view, certainly, it has been more than anything else the repeated interactions with Don, and the force of his arguments, that have kept me thinking critically about my own views on these matters.

Don Garrett: Thanks very much, Peter. That was very fair. What I am about to say about reason and induction, which has already been partly described by Peter, has been much improved through interaction with him. He got me to abandon a formulation of it that was in my book and that was unduly narrow. We've been discussing this at Hume conferences for about fifteen years now, and we do have a general principle that anything we can agree on is generally right. [laughter] And there are getting to be more and more things. As Peter said, my view is that reason for Hume is the faculty of reasoning, that is, the faculty of making inferences. There are two kinds of such reasoning for Hume: *demonstrative reasoning*, which establishes things with certainty and makes the denial of the conclusions inconceivable, prevalent in mathematics, and then there's everything else, which is called *probable reasoning* and turns out to be dependent on experience. That this is his way of understanding 'reason' is shown in particular by his common interchanges of 'things due to reason' and 'things due to reasoning', by his terms 'demonstrative reasoning' and 'probable reasoning' as names for sub-faculties of reason, and especially by his repeated form of argument: 'if not by demonstrative reason and not by probable reason, then not done by reason.' That occurs in several topics in Hume – at least three topics, one of which is induction. It is also shown by his treatment 'Of the reason of animals' [*Treatise* 1.3.16], which is about the inferences that animals make. This is a somewhat narrow use of the term 'reason', narrower than some other uses of the term 'reason' at the time, uses that Peter will describe, some of which are somewhat honorific, or opposed to 'faith', for example: reason vs. faith. But it is, I think, Locke's official sense, so I'm invoking a feature of Locke's view here. I think Locke was very influential on Hume on this particular sort of topic: the terminology and delineation of epistemic faculties.

You also see it in James Beattie, responding directly to Hume. Beattie distinguishes four senses of the term 'reason', but the fourth sense is that of 'those who are most accurate in distinguishing' [Beattie 1770, pp. 32-33]: they use 'reason' as the name of the faculty for making inferences. Beattie says that's the sense in which he will use it, as the term for the faculty of inference. That sense is common throughout the history of philosophy, as are others; so far, we each have instances to cite. Reason in this sense is an important object of study in the science of man, which is what Hume proposes to be doing, and he is studying that process. He is especially studying probable inference, which he thinks has not been sufficiently examined, and which he claims depends on the relation of cause and effect (which we will discuss later). The relation of cause and effect then depends in turn on experience of constant conjunctions, that is: two things going together. You see one thing following another enough times, and then you see one and you project that the other will also occur. Reason, as Hume conceives it, is a function, surprisingly, of the *imagination* in one broad sense of that term. He has two senses of the term 'imagination'. Imagination in the broad sense is just the faculty of having ideas that are not memories. So anything that happens with ideas, the production of ideas, the production of ideas of various kinds in various circumstances, including ideas that are believed, is a function of the imagination in that broad sense. He introduces a narrower sense of 'imagination', which is the same thing 'excluding only our demonstrative and probable reasonings' [*Treatise* 1.3.9.19n and 2.2.7.6n]. In that narrower sense, then, reason is *opposed* to imagination, while in the broader sense reason is just another function of the imagination. The key puzzle that Peter was describing could be put this way: Hume says that there are 'inferences', or 'reasonings' (Hume uses both terms), that are 'not determin'd by reason', or 'founded on reasoning or any process of the understanding'. What could it mean to say that there are reasonings that are not determined by reason? I think he intends a conclusion in what we would now call cognitive psychology, about the causation of probable reasonings. In his conclusion about these particular inferences from experience, as elsewhere, 'determined' means: 'caused by'. So probable inferences, reasonings, exertions of reason, are not themselves produced by a process of mediating reasoning or inference. They *are* reasonings, all right; they just aren't produced by a mediating piece of reasoning.

I think that the best way to see this is just to let the argument itself show you what the conclusion is supposed to mean. Here's how the argument works: Hume points out that when we start making inferences from experience, what we have is experience of past constant conjunctions, plus a current impression, a sensation, or a memory. That's where we start, and where we end up is with a belief in the occurrence of a new or further instance of a kind of thing that has been constantly conjoined with experienced objects like the one that is currently occupying our mind. So there's a sort of gap there from an experience of past constant conjunctions of A and B, plus a current A, to a belief in another B. He variously describes that transition as 'putting trust in past experience', 'presupposing the uniformity of nature', and 'making the presupposition that the future will resemble the past'. That's the name of a little task, of a crucial transition that the mind makes, and the question is: how does the mind manage to make that transition? Here's one theory he considers and rejects: perhaps it does it by *reason*.

Hume says: if reason determined us to make these inferences, it would 'proceed upon the principle' that nature is uniform. For what does reason do, after all? It produces conclusions by reasoning;

it gives you a belief as the result of reasoning. So if reason is what engages us to make this transitional move, it would have to do it by giving us a *belief* that nature was uniform, which we would then *combine* with our past experience and our current impression and arrive at the ultimate conclusion in the new thing that we are now believing. The structure of his argument is: if that *were* how we did it, by reason giving us a belief about the uniformity of nature, then the belief would have to result from either demonstrative reasoning or probable reasoning. Those are the only two kinds of reasoning. And yet it can't possibly come from either kind of reasoning. I won't go through the argument that eliminates those two kinds of reasoning, but it's a *really* good argument. That's part of why this argument was so famous; even when people didn't agree what the conclusion was, they could see that that bit was a really good bit. Hume's conclusion is that we don't make this transition by reasoning at all. We don't do it by getting a belief as the result of reasoning about the uniformity of nature. We do it in some other way, without a belief in the uniformity of nature. We do *presuppose* the uniformity of nature, but that just means we *act as though* we were taking nature to be uniform, even though we don't formulate that belief. Instead, the positive answer to 'how do we presuppose the uniformity of nature' is that we do it as a result of a mechanism called custom or habit, which is a feature of the imagination in the narrower sense. That's the general mechanism by which things that are repeated many times then occur again without any further thought about them. It's the same mechanism that makes you brush your teeth at night. The first time, you might have given yourself a little argument, but now it's just custom or habit.

Reason then has a kind of requisite sub-operation, this key transition that's due to another faculty, the imagination. You might think of it as a subcontractor. Reason needs this transition made. It can't make it by producing a belief in the uniformity of nature itself, so custom or habit performs the operation instead. An analogous point holds for 'the senses', which is our ability to get a belief in external bodies as a result of sensation. That process is what Hume calls an operation of 'the senses', but there is a particular crucial step in it, which is performed not by the senses but by the imagination in the narrow sense – that is, something to do with operations with ideas that are not reasoning [*Treatise* 1.4.2.4-14]. In the same way, the customary transition that Hume describes in induction is due not to reason, but to the imagination in that narrow sense of some feature of ideas that is not itself demonstrative or probable reasoning.

As a claim in cognitive psychology, this is not itself an epistemic evaluation. It's not telling you whether you should believe the inductive conclusion or not. It's not saying whether it's good or bad. But the claim does have logical implications and psychological consequences. It implies that a belief in the uniformity of nature couldn't achieve worthiness to be believed, epistemic merit I'd say, through being produced by reasoning that's *independent* of presupposing the uniformity of nature, because Hume has shown that it can't be produced that way at all. It therefore can't get any warrant for being believed *through* being produced in that way. It can't be produced in that way, and that seems disappointing. It feels like an 'infirmity' in our faculties, and it can contribute to an overall lessening of your degree of belief about things. When you recognize: 'I thought maybe I would be able to do that sort of thing by reasoning, but I guess not', that diminishes your own self-assessment just a bit. It also lends itself to an argument, which he offers in the *Enquiry*, that probable reasoning, induction, is a kind of *instinct* in a way and, like other instincts, may be fallacious [*Enquiry* 12.22]. You might notice that that is itself a sort of inductive argument: many instincts have been found to be fallacious; this one's an instinct; so it too might prove to be fallacious, based on past experience. It doesn't imply that the belief that nature is uniform lacks *epistemic merit*, though, or that it's something that *shouldn't* be believed, or in fact that it isn't something that is probably true. It's only a view about the lack of a reasoned belief in the uniformity of nature *as part of the origin* of our probable inferences. The belief in the uniformity of nature isn't something that people arrive at *before* engaging in induction. Given that they have already begun to engage in induction, however, they can use induction to reflect that nature *has* been uniform in the *past*, so it will probably be uniform in the *future*. That argument doesn't explain why they are inductive beings; they wouldn't *appreciate* that argument unless they were *already* inductive beings who were *already* 'presupposing the uniformity of nature'. But given that they *are* that kind of being, they can come to formulate that belief; and in fact, I think Hume thinks it's not just pragmatically acceptable to think that nature is uniform I think he thinks it's *probably true* – that may be something stronger than what Peter thinks Hume believes about it; we'll see.

One final question: is the claim true? I could talk about that for a long time, but I'll just say 'yes'... [laughter] ... Hume was exactly right. So for a long time there was this famous argument, which people felt was a great argument, but of course its conclusion was preposterous and false. I think it's a great argument whose conclusion, understood the way I understand it, is important and true.

PM: Thank you very much, Don. Now, I'm going to oppose Don's interpretation in various ways, but I'm not going to oppose everything he says. On the Uniformity Principle, for example, I think we're absolutely at one. Likewise on custom and habit and so forth. The big difference between us is: what does Hume mean by 'reason'? And therefore, what is the actual import of his conclusion? Now, what I want to suggest is that reason for Hume is the overall cognitive faculty, so it's not just the faculty of inference. It's the faculty for discovery, discernment, or judgement of truth and falsehood.

To back that up, I'll start by citing a few quotations from people of the time. The first is from Richard Price's *Review of Morals*; I put him first just because he's not Francis Hutcheson ... [laughter] ... 'the power within us that *understands*; ... the faculty ... that discerns *truth*, that views, compares, and *judges* of all ideas and things' is then identified with *reason* (and contrasted with *sense*) [Price 1758, pp. 20-1]. Next we have Francis Hutcheson saying a similar thing in his *Illustrations on the Moral Sense*: 'Reason is understood to denote our *Power of finding out true Propositions*' [Hutcheson 1742, p. 215]. Shortly after this, Hutcheson outlines what he takes to be the standardly received faculty structure: at the top level we have *reason* 'presenting the natures and relations of things', alongside *the will* which disposes us to act on what is presented as good or evil; then below these we have the *senses* which 'answer to' *reason* (also called *the understanding*), and *the passions* which 'answer to' *the will* [Hutcheson 1742, pp. 219-20]. It's striking that in four different works, either published or revised in 1742, Hutcheson inserted this sort of point on the structure of the faculties. In 1740, he had received Hume's *Treatise*, and I just wonder when he says: 'Writers on these subjects should remember the common Divisions of the Faculties of the Soul' [*ibid.*], whether he might partly have been rapping Hume over the knuckles for playing fast and loose with reason and the imagination!

This standard faculty structure involves a general divide between what we now call the *cognitive* and the *conative* realms. So you've got *reason* and *the will*, where reason – also often called *the understanding* – basically perceives and judges the deliverances of the subordinate faculties (such as the senses) to discover, as Hutcheson puts it: 'the natures and relations of things'. And once reason has discovered what is true, the will then makes decisions accordingly, depending upon what we want. So we've got a general distinction between the truth-finding faculty or faculties, and the purpose-giving side. And this is absolutely common to authors of that time: David Hartley, for example, says 'The *Understanding* is that Faculty, by which we ... pursue Truth, and assent to, or dissent from Propositions' [Hartley 1749, p. iii]. Now if we take a look at what Hume says about reason, we can see that it very much matches with this. I'm going to quote a passage from the *Treatise* and one from each of the three works that developed out of the *Treatise*, which he described as 'recast' versions. In chronological order: 'Reason is the discovery of truth or falshood' [*Treatise* 3.1.1.9]; 'that faculty, by which we discern Truth and Falshood' [*Enquiry* 1.4 n., 1748/50 editions]; 'Thus the distinct boundaries and offices of reason and of taste are easily ascertained. The former conveys the knowledge of truth and falsehood' [1751, Appendix 1.21]; 'reason, in a strict sense, as meaning the judgment of truth and falshood' [1757, 5.1]. They all look pretty unambiguous, and they fit closely with what people at the time are saying. Here's another quotation from the *Treatise* [Appendix, paragraph 1]: 'There is nothing I wou'd more willingly lay hold of, than an opportunity of confessing my errors; and shou'd esteem such a return to truth and reason to be more honourable than the most unerring judgment'. And there are various other places where Hume puts truth and reason together. So to sum up my first main point: usage at the time sees *reason* as the overarching cognitive faculty, with other subordinate faculties 'answering' or reporting to it. Thus the imagination, the memory, and the senses all report to reason, and reason makes the judgement of what is true and false.

My second line of argument is to do with reason and the understanding. Now, Don appealed to John Locke, whose most famous work is the *Essay concerning Human Understanding*; and this term 'human understanding' is used relatively uncontroversially by a whole host of people in a very broad sense. Like Locke's *Essay*, we also have Hume's *Enquiry concerning Human Understanding*, and Book 1 of the *Treatise*, entitled 'Of the Understanding'. But then in that same Book we have lots of passages where Hume apparently treats 'reason' and 'the understanding' as absolutely equivalent. Some of these are:

> ... the next question is, Whether experience produces the idea by means of *the understanding* or of the imagination; whether we are determin'd by *reason* to make the transition, or by a certain association and relation of perceptions. [*Treatise* 1.3.6.4, my emphasis]

Here he's using 'the understanding' early in the sentence and then he's referring back to it using the word 'reason'.

> ... the mind ... is not determin'd by *reason*, but by certain principles, which associate together the ideas of these objects, and unite them in *the imagination*. Had ideas no more union in *the fancy* than objects seem to have to *the understanding*, ... [*Treatise* 1.3.6.12, my emphasis]

Just as he's oscillating between the words 'imagination' and 'fancy' purely for the sake of elegant variation – I think it's uncontroversial that the imagination and fancy are just different names for one and the same faculty – I think the same is clearly true here of 'reason' and 'the understanding'. There are at least two dozen Humean passages in a similar spirit [e.g. from *Treatise* 1.4.1.1, 1.4.2.46, 1.4.2.57], but perhaps the most interesting are a pair of footnotes, one of which was originally placed in Book 2 of the *Treatise*:

> ... when it [the imagination] is oppos'd to the understanding, I understand the same faculty, excluding only our demonstrative and probable reasonings. [*Treatise* 2.2.7.6n]

Hume decided to move this into Book 1 while the *Treatise* was in press, and when he came to do so I think that he looked at it and thought it was a bit inelegant – 'the understanding, I understand' – so he changed the wording, replacing 'the understanding' with 'reason':

> ... when I oppose it [the imagination] to reason, I mean the same faculty, excluding only our demonstrative and probable reasonings. [*Treatise* 1.3.9.19n]

So again, it looks as though he thinks of 'reason' and 'the understanding' as completely interchangeable. Now if they are interchangeable, then that is a strong argument for a broad reading of *reason* as the cognitive faculty as whole, rather than just inference.

I also think this fits the logic of Hume's arguments. Don has appealed to the *Treatise* argument on induction, but I think that's the only one of the big arguments which really favours his interpretation. In the *Treatise*, Hume says, in effect: 'the Uniformity Principle can't be founded on demonstrative reasoning; it can't be founded on probable reasoning; therefore it can't be founded on reason' – and as Don points out, that rather makes it look as though reason just is *demonstrative reasoning* and *probable reasoning*. But in the *Enquiry* version, he also explicitly rules out intuition (twice) and I think he also deliberately rules out appeal to what the senses deliver (at quite some length), which suggests a broader view of reason. Another of his famous arguments is in *Treatise* 1.4.2, on the external world, and contains passages like this:

> This sentiment, then, as it is entirely unreasonable, must proceed from some other faculty than the understanding. ... So that upon the whole our reason neither does... [*Treatise* 1.4.2.14]

Again we've got 'the understanding' and 'reason' being interchanged. But notice that he's saying that because 'this sentiment' is unreasonable, it can't come from reason.

> ... 'tis a false opinion ... and consequently ... can never arise from reason ... [*Treatise* 1.4.2.43]

Again it looks as though reason is the *cognitive* faculty – it's the faculty by which we discern truth and falsehood. It's not just the faculty of argument. Going back to the *Enquiry* version of the induction argument, I find it quite significant to compare this with a passage from the *Letter from a Gentleman to his Friend in Edinburgh*, which Hume wrote in 1745 at the same time as he was working on the Enquiry (which came out in 1748). He was in the country, and says in the letter words to the effect 'sorry I haven't got the *Treatise* with me so I can't quote page numbers, but let me outline the way these things are generally seen'. Then we get this:

> It is common for Philosophers to distinguish the Kinds of Evidence into *intuitive, demonstrative, sensible,* and *moral*; ... [1745, paragraph 26]

'Moral' reasoning is *probable* reasoning; 'sensible' evidence is *sensory* evidence. And those four types of evidence match up exactly with what he's ruling out as potential supports of the Uniformity Principle in Section 4 of the *Enquiry*. So, in other words, I think that here Hume is seeing reason as the cognitive faculty, which handles the four different types of evidence, and he's knocking out each of those in turn.

Now if we examine the conclusion of the famous argument about induction, Don and I are actually both agreed, I think, that this statement from the *Enquiry* is the most authoritative:

> in all reasonings from experience, there is a step taken by the mind, which is not supported by any argument or process of the understanding [*Enquiry* 5.2]

DG: It's a good one.

PM: Again we have a phrase, 'not supported by any argument', which sounds rather more epistemological than psychological. And 'not supported by any ... process of the understanding' – so Hume is not only ruling out inference, by the looks of things. And I think Don has a bit of a difficulty here, especially when we bear in mind that there are plenty of passages in Hume's works where he refers to bad arguments [e.g. *Treatise* 1.2.4.11, 1.3.3.5 7, 1.3.6.9 10, 1.4.5.30; 1779, 9.2, 4, 11]. The point is that if Hume is doing what Don takes him to be doing, then he is trying to show that the Uniformity Principle is not, as a matter of cognitive psychology, founded on an *argument*, a *stepwise inference*. But in fact, he never deals with the case of a *bad* stepwise inference. If his hypothesis is what Don thinks, then he surely has to rule out the possibility of the Uniformity Principle's being based on a *bad* argument. But he doesn't even consider it. Now Don said – this was from earlier on – that according to Hume, there are only two kinds of reasoning: demonstrative reasoning and probable reasoning. But, in that case, Hume's taxonomy has left out an awful lot because it has left out, for example, bad demonstrative arguments. These don't count as genuinely demonstrative because they're fallacious. But they're not probable arguments either. And Hume, it seems to me, is in various places [*ibid.*] quite clearly saying that there are would-be demonstrative arguments which genuinely count as *arguments*, but which are bad. And as construed by Don, Hume wouldn't have ruled these out as possible sources for belief in the Uniformity Principle. So his argument, I think, would be seriously incomplete if he meant what Don takes him to mean.

On the nature of Hume's 'scepticism' that results from his famous argument, I think Don and I are very broadly agreed and I must acknowledge here a debt to him because in the Monterey debate that we had, and in the paper that came from that [Garrett 1998], Don drew attention to a very important passage from the beginning of Section 12 in the *Enquiry concerning Human Understanding*, where Hume talks about different kinds of scepticism. He says that if you doubt your faculties right from the start (so-called *antecedent* scepticism), if you're not prepared to accept your faculties at all without a proof that they're reliable, then you've had it, because without your faculties you've got nothing to do the proof with. And he goes on to say that we should only adopt a kind of *consequent* scepticism, which is that we give default authority to our faculties until we've found a problem with them. Now I think that's dead right. It's now quite a keystone of my interpretation – and I'm grateful to Don for having drawn attention to that passage. So my line would be that 'reason', for Hume, is our default cognitive faculty. It has these four different types of evidence, and Hume is showing that none of them can lead to the Uniformity Principle. Like Don, I think it's a good argument – but for slightly different reasons.

DG: We want to let people get a chance to ask questions, so I'll limit myself to making a couple of statements. I don't agree with everything Peter said. I grant that Hume roughly interchanges the terms 'reason' and 'understanding' in his writing. In fact in the *Treatise*, there is a passage I mentioned [*Treatise* 1.3.9.19n)] in which he distinguishes *reason* from imagination in the narrow sense as being our *demonstrative and probable reasonings*. But that's an almost exact replica of a footnote he had earlier placed elsewhere in the *Treatise* [*Treatise* 2.2.7.6n], which says that imagination in the narrow sense is everything that is covered by imagination in the broad sense except demonstrative and probable reasoning, *which is what constitutes 'the understanding'*. So there he characterises the understanding, too, as just being our demonstrative and probable reasonings. The understanding generally involves the intuition of self-evident truths as well as reasoning, but in many cases the difference between those two doesn't really matter. In Locke, you had a broad sense of 'understanding' and a narrow sense of 'reason', set out in a chapter called 'Of Reason' within a book called *An Essay Concerning Human Understanding*. Peter thinks reason for Hume *blew up* to cover everything that the Lockean understanding did, while I think that in Hume the understanding shrank down to encompass only what reason did, plus intuition. The view of a master cognitive faculty that's a sort of spectator I think is the wrong way to think about cognition for Hume – it's not a way he'd think about it given that he doesn't really have a mental spectator, he's just got a mind that is a bundle of perceptions. In Locke, 'understanding' is defined as (i) the having of ideas, which is now done by the imagination for Hume; *plus* (ii) understanding the signification of signs, which Hume says is really just a kind of probable causal reasoning; *plus* (iii) inference, or the perception of relations among ideas. So I think there's a natural story of how the understanding gets to be roughly equivalent to reason in Hume. I would note that Hume always distinguishes both memory and the senses from the understanding and at no point includes them in the understanding. Peter has a reading of the *Enquiry* argument about induction according to which sensation *is* included in the understanding there, but I don't think that's right. I think Hume's reference to sensation is part of what I called 'the set-up', explaining what we have before the transition occurs. It's not playing a role in the explanation *of* the transition, and the statement that Hume gives at the very end of that section of what his conclusion has been doesn't mention sensation at all, but only 'argument'.

Hume certainly does say that reason is something that enables us to discern truth and falsehood, but he doesn't generally say that it's the *only* source. Memory, too, lets us know about truth and falsehood, for example. Reason, he wants to emphasise, *concerns* truth and falsehood and not, for example, the rightness and wrongness of actions themselves. He does describe it at one point as 'the discovery of truth and falsehood', but he has already said that reasoning is always a 'discovery of relations' – so it's a particular *way* of getting truth and falsehood that's a 'discovery' (that is, an 'uncovering') in a way that memory and sensation aren't a discovery. Moreover, Hume calls reason the discovery and truth and falsehood in the very same section [*Treatise* 3.1.1] in which he says that moral distinctions are not made by reason. Why not? Because they're not made by *demonstrative reasoning* and they're not made by *probable reasoning*. I don't think 'supported by' is necessarily a term of epistemic evaluation for Hume. It's like his general term 'foundation'— a term he also uses in this connection — which is often very causal rather than epistemic. For example, superstition is 'founded on' fear.

'Inference' or 'reasoning' doesn't mean just *any* mental transition to assent; for example, Hume thinks sheer repetition in education gets you to assent, and that's a kind of mental transition, but it's not inference or reasoning. I think he really thinks that only demonstration and probable reasoning qualify as kinds of reasoning. He sometimes talks about 'pretended' demonstrations that are not really demonstrations and are not fully demonstrative reasonings, and he remarks that 'demonstrations may be difficult to be comprehended but can never have such difficulties as will weaken their authority once they are comprehended'. That suggests that when you do understand genuine demonstrative reasoning, then you see that it can't be wrong. Probable reasonings on the other hand can be bad. But all probable reasonings, good ones and bad ones, fall within the scope of Hume's argument that all probable reasonings presuppose the uniformity of nature in a way that can't be accounted for by any probable reasoning.

Having said all this, here are two points of agreement – so things that must be entirely right! I think we agree that the understanding, which is roughly reason – however big or small that is – has a *proprietary* function of reasoning, that is, it itself accounts for reasoning, and, as you put it, it takes input from the senses and memory....

PM: Absolutely.

DG: ... I agree that reasoning operates on deliverances of the senses and memory – that's part of Hume's account of how probable reasoning is possible. So we agree about that. We're disagreeing about whether reason *encompasses* them by doing that. We also both agree that reason, or the understanding, can be subjected to criticism, and it is not just by *definition* a truth-generating faculty, so that it makes sense to ask whether we should rely on it, and whether it is or is not giving us the truth. We agree that it has a kind of *default authority*: you begin by being entitled to operate with it. But I think Peter's view is that it is only by being part of the big understanding that a faculty can have that authority, for Hume, whereas I think that all of our belief-generating mechanisms – memory, the senses and reason in his narrow sense – all have that default authority themselves, so that they don't have to get it from a larger understanding.

PM: I don't want to hold up the questions, so I'm just very quickly going to answer a couple of small points you made, Don. Yes, we agree on the reporting to – but I'm not adopting the view that reason for Hume is some kind of spectator. It's perhaps worth making that clear. Hutcheson hints at this faculty of ratiocination, so that when you're constructing an argument it seems that you've got a sub-faculty that's mixing your ideas around in such a way that you can see their relations, and reason is just a kind of viewer. Hume certainly doesn't take that line. So, as you said, we agree that reasoning is a sort of proprietary function of reason proper.

DG: So there's reason not to think he's so Hutchesonian.

PM: The other point here concerns the relation between reason and the imagination – this is very tricky. Don was talking about the imagination playing the role as a subcontractor, as it were, for reason. Now I think that's wrong. I think that's making the faculties real entities in a way that Hume's philosophy ought not to allow, because he's very critical about faculty language if it claims to be explanatory. The way I'd go – and this is in some ways very similar to Don's view but subtly different, I think – is that when he says inductive inference depends on the imagination (as he does in the *Treatise*, though not in the *Enquiry*), what he means is not that reason is trying to do this inference and the imagination says 'Oh! You can't do that by yourself – let me lend a hand ...' No, what he means is that there is a sub-process *in our reasoning faculty*, which is imagination-like, which is not itself *cognitive*. It involves extrapolation, going beyond anything that we have cognised. And that, I think, is the way to understand Hume's view. Now I think that when we iron all these things out, there's not so much that separates Don and me on this, but there is a bit.

DG: So, one sentence – and then maybe you'll do one word, and then one syllable, and then we'll each do a letter... [Laughter] It's fair enough to say that you don't have to have judgement, the understanding, be a spectator, but I'm also not treating imagination and reason as talking to each other on the subcontractor model. Rather, my view is that if you want to know the answer to the question 'was something done by reason as opposed to imagination in the narrow sense', ask yourself: 'was it produced by demonstrative or probable reasoning?' If not, then it's not due to reason. And that's why the imagination in the narrow sense is performing the customary transition. I would say that an advantage of my interpretation is that I don't just have to say that that transition is 'imagination-like'; I can say it was done, as Hume says, by the imagination.

PM: 'Wrong!' I'm only allowed one word, right? [Laughter]

SM: Are you ready to turn it over to the rest of us? Well, let me just ask you who or what reasons or has understanding and how far your interpretations imply or depend on a sense of self or identity (which we know also in Book 1 of the *Treatise* is coming under scrutiny by the epistemological argument and the inductive method)? Is there a difference in how your approaches would deal with that question? You've had a lot of talk about reason, about the faculties, about reasoning – does there have to be, or what would it look like to be, the self that does that reasoning?

DG: I think we're probably on the same page about that – we'll see. I think we agree that Hume's conception of the self or the mind is that it's a bundle of perceptions; it is perceptions themselves, ideas and impressions, in causal relations with one another. There is no separate soul, no substance in which these perceptions inhere, no standing-aside spectator – which is not to say that ideas of ideas don't occur. Ideas of ideas do occur, but those are not viewed by a spectator. In that sense it's a 'no-spectator' view. In order to explain why the mind has the powers that it does — and we've talked about faculties — I think we agree that Hume is quite happy to infer in general from *A does something*, to *A has a power for doing it*, to *A has a faculty for doing it*. That involves not treating powers as individual agents to whom things are to be ascribed. Locke makes a big point of denying that powers are 'agents', by which he means: things act *because* of their powers, *through* their powers; it's not the *powers* that act. Powers are not doers of things; things that have powers are doers of things with the powers that they have. So wherever you can find something being done, there's a power or a faculty of doing it. It belongs to the self or the mind, which in the first instance is this system of interrelated perceptions. But I think Hume is quite clear that it requires a physiological under-structure, a brain, to make these kinds of processes possible. He discusses that at some points. The only other thing I would say is that the argument about induction we are discussing is an argument that Hume gives before he tells you what he thinks the self is. In that sense, it shouldn't *depend* on his view of the self – but it should be *consistent* with it.

PM: I would just add it's also an argument he continues to give long after he has lost confidence in his view of personal identity. This is quite a big difference between us. I think Don's reading of the *Treatise* view is more or less correct ... I agree pretty much with it, barring a few details. But the fact is that Hume openly despaired of his theory of personal identity in October 1740, barely twenty-one months after he'd first published it, and it doesn't appear again. So I take the view that his later works are more authoritative. But, certainly, the argument had better be independent of that. Just one point I'd pick you up on, Don, is that I take Hume and Locke to be far less in favour of faculties than you do, I think. You said that if X does A, then X must have a power for A, which means X has a faculty for doing A. That implies straight away that I've got a faculty for producing bad would-be demonstrative arguments. I agree with you that such bad arguments are not demonstrative, just as I might say to a logic student, 'that's not a deduction', meaning that's not a *valid* deduction. That doesn't stop it being an *argument*. So if there are bad arguments, then we must have a faculty for producing bad arguments by the reasoning you just gave. So where does that belong then? Not part of reason, apparently, according to you. Well, I can quite happily exclude it from a proper functioning *cognitive* faculty. But it's not clear to me that you can exclude it if the faculty of reason is just the faculty of producing an argument. Here is an argument, and it's been produced.

DG: It certainly is being *taken* as an argument and there are processes of inference that are going on as *part* of it, and then there's also a bad part. The bad part is not some demonstration. It's due to the imagination in the narrow sense. That's my view and I'm sticking with it. [Laughter]

Q: I'm just wondering if you could say more how Lockean Hume is about reason. I mean, I'm thinking here about some of the arguments we find in Locke's letters to Stillingfleet, where he gave a better sense of how far the scope of reason can go. You find a better picture of what Locke thinks about substances, for instance, in his letters to Stillingfleet, where he says that equality cannot exist by itself but we need to supply some substratum or some support. Reason can give us this idea of the support but I'm not sure Hume would be willing to accept that...

DG: Yes, Hume offers a criticism of Locke on a similar point. Locke has an account of the origin of the idea of power in the *Essay* according to which, if you read it the way Hume read it, you basically infer your way to having an idea of power from things that you observe. And Hume, I think quite astutely, notes that Locke himself had made it a principle in the *Essay* that you could never acquire any new simple idea from reasoning. So if you're proposing acquiring an idea just from reasoning, Hume certainly doesn't think you can do that, and Locke shouldn't think you can do that. Hume thinks he has discovered that all non-demonstrative reasoning depends on this mechanism of induction, and that provides him with a way of delineating certain things as not capable of being produced by reasoning – because if it were probable reasoning you would have had experience of the one and of the other, constantly conjoined, and if you don't have that, then there can't be reasoning there. That might be overly strict, but that is his line.

Q: This is directed to Peter. You began with these quotations about reason being a truth-finding faculty, which you found in common between Hume and some others in the eighteenth century ... I wasn't quite sure what the point of putting Hutcheson in was. Is it because, in fact, he is writing prior to Hume (although you have a quotation from a later edition) ...

PM: As I mentioned, it's quite interesting that his four things that say most about the faculties are all dated 1742. One of them is the *Synopsis of Metaphysics*, another is his *Short Introduction to Moral Philosophy*, and the other two are a footnote and a paragraph in later editions of works of his. So I was speculating that it might even be that contact with Hume's *Treatise* caused him to do that...

Q: It could be for the *Illustrations on the Moral Sense*, but I doubt it would for the *Synopsis*, which is almost certainly written fifteen years earlier.

PM: It's hard to know because he added extra stuff in the other works so maybe he did in the *Synopsis* – who knows?

Q: The *Synopsis* was printed without his permission – he hadn't passed it for press.

PM: OK, thanks – that's a useful point, I'll remember it.

Q: Anyway, that's not the main point I wanted to bring up. It is that if you simply look at the logic teaching of the period, now this is strictly logic, logic as a curriculum subject in colleges, I'm pretty certain you will find it in the logic dictates that Hume would have had. Undoubtedly the apprehension of truth is seen as the sole aim of logic, which proceeds by *ratio*. And there must be a legacy of that in Hume's mind because this was drummed into him in the first week he studied philosophy in college.

PM: The Introduction to the *Treatise* suggests that Hume saw Book 1 as a contribution to logic: 'The sole end of logic is to explain the principles and operations of our reasoning faculty, and the nature of our ideas: Morals and criticism regard our taste and sentiments' [*Treatise*,

Introduction 5]. It looks like he's describing the contents of the *Treatise*. Now on that reckoning, *logic* is basically to do with the *understanding*. And, of course, Locke's *Essay* was called *logic* by lots of people at the time ('facultative logic' and all that), so I don't find that a problem. And we shouldn't be misled by the term 'our reasoning faculty': today, we naturally use the word 'reasoning' and we think of stepwise inference. But if you look in Johnson's *Dictionary* of 1756, all you get on reasoning is that, basically, it's the operation of *reason*. If you're looking for words that mean stepwise inference, it's not 'reasoning', but 'deduction' or 'ratiocination'. And it's not 'argument' either, because if you look at how Johnson talks about 'argument', it's a *ground of assent*. So when we read Hume and see him saying 'there is no argument' of some kind, and we think that must mean *ratiocination* – no, it doesn't! At least, not according to Johnson's *Dictionary* and other sources. So I think it's very dangerous to take these words and read them in the modern sense and assume they're the same at that time. Anyway, I'm interested in that point about Hutcheson – I must chase that up! That's grist to my mill. But the reason I quoted Hutcheson was partly because, obviously, Hutcheson was a big influence on Hume, Hume knew him and so on, which makes it relevant; but the main thing is that his *Synopsis* is by far the most explicit thing I was able to find. I would be interested to take your advice on other things that I could find.

Q: I think the logic tradition will give you plenty of ammunition, but it may be at the wrong point because they introduce reason right at the very beginning when the first faculty of reason is the simple apprehension.

PM: No, that's fine. That's grist to my mill.

SM: Do we have time to move on to causation?

DG: Well, I might suggest that I could do the introduction and you could present, and then I would waive my response and go directly to questions – inasmuch as I agree with most things you say but would add things to them.

PM: We could do that.

DG: Hume regards the relation of cause and effect as the master relation through which we try both to understand the world and to achieve our ends in it. His attempt to 'fully explain' it constitutes one of his best-known and most important contributions to philosophy. Yet the wealth of arguments and claims he offers have led to vigorously competing interpretations of what that explanation is – a competition that has come to reach a peak in recent years.

On the one hand, Hume offers what he calls a 'precise definition' of 'cause' in terms of 'constant conjunction' (that is, the regularities we were talking about). Here's the definition: 'an object precedent and contiguous to another, and where all objects resembling the former are placed in like relations of precedency and contiguity to those objects, that resemble the latter' [*Treatise* 1.3.14.30-31]. He goes on to cite and employ this definition, along with a second definition in terms of mental association and inference, as an important part of his philosophical method. Thus, it seems that he is a reductionist, reducing the relation of cause and effect, by a method of meaning analysis, to nothing more than what he calls 'constant conjunction' between pairs of successive objects or events. This has come to be called the 'Old Hume' interpretation.

Yet on the other hand, he goes on to allow that our ideas of this relation are 'imperfect' and that both definitions may 'be esteem'd defective, because drawn from objects foreign to the cause' [*Treatise* 1.3.14.31]; moreover, he alludes variously to 'the power by which one object produces another' [*Treatise* 1.3.1.1], the 'internal structure or operating principle of objects' [*Treatise* 1.3.14.29], and 'the ultimate connexion of ... objects', concluding that 'we can never penetrate so far into the essence and construction of bodies, as to perceive the principle, on which their mutual influence depends' [*Treatise* 2.3.1.4] and that, more generally, 'we cannot penetrate into the reason of the conjunction' [*Treatise* 1.3.6.15]. Thus, he seems to be a realist (though maybe a sceptical realist) about causation, allowing that there are or at least may be real—even if inaccessible to us – causal powers and relations that go beyond constant conjunction and our subsequent inference and mental association. This interpretation – which first blazed into new prominence (it's not an entirely new interpretation) in the 1980s with books by John P. Wright [1983] and Galen Strawson [1989], among others – has come to be called the 'New Hume' interpretation and has often seemed on the verge of becoming a new orthodoxy.

On yet a third hand (you didn't know there were three hands!), however, Hume also holds that a 'necessary connexion' is required as an 'essential ... part' of the relation of cause and effect [*Treatise* 1.3.6.3]. And his endeavour to discover the nature of our idea of this necessary connection and its experiential source in an 'impression' is what leads him to his two definitions; and at the end of that search, he declares that what we take to be such a 'necessity and power [lying] in the objects' is in fact merely an internal feeling of 'the determination of the mind, to pass from the idea of an object to that of its usual attendant', a feeling that the mind erroneously treats as a quality of the objects observed [*Treatise* 1.3.14.25] even though the ideas derived from this feeling of determination 'represent not any thing, that does or can belong to the objects' [*Treatise* 1.3.14.19]. Thus, it also seems that he denies that there are any such things as genuine causal relations of any kind in nature and is instead a projectivist, admitting only fictitious projections of internal sentiments onto objects that cannot genuinely be qualified by them and also, perhaps, expressions of our own mental dispositions to make inductive inferences. This might properly be called the 'Other Hume' interpretation, which has been developed and defended most recently by Simon Blackburn [1993], Helen Beebee [2006], and Angela Coventry [2006].

Peter has weighed in on this debate with two papers, one in a collection on the New Hume debate [2007] and another first presented at a conference I co-directed in New York which was then published in *Mind* [2009], that constitute, I think, the most devastating case yet offered in defence of the Old Hume against the New. At the same time, I have been endeavouring to split the interpretive difference among proponents of the various Humes – offering conciliatory compromises to each and, perhaps, satisfying none. [Laughter] Still, I am hopeful that we, Peter and I, can, at least on some points, join forces. So I'll let him loose his artilleries.

PM: Don and I agree about a lot when it comes to causation and Don's made some very interesting contributions on the interpretation of the two definitions and offers these conciliatory nuances – but, unfortunately, we're not going to be able to go there because we're just going to have to concentrate on the big, rather crude picture.

Traditionally, Hume's been seen as a reductionist about causation, someone who says causation just ultimately comes down to regularities. And some people then say that he denies necessary connections. But he can't do both! If he's a reductionist, if he thinks causation is a matter of regularities, then he *does* believe in necessary connections – but he thinks they just come down to regularities. That often puzzles people because they say that's *not* what we mean by 'necessity'. But Hume has another argument saying that this is what we mean by necessity; indeed it's all we can mean. Now you may think it's a crazy argument – and this is where I will put my cards on the table: I don't think Hume is right, but I think it's what he meant. And I think it's pretty provable that this is what he meant. But against this, a lot of the argument for the New Hume goes like this: 'Look, here's Hume referring again and again to causes and powers and so forth. He must believe there are real causes and powers so he can't be a reductionist.' Sorry, he *does* believe in real causes and powers: but they're to be interpreted in a reductionist manner. At least, that seems to be the obvious way of reading him.

Hume starts from the empiricist assumption which he gets from Locke, and I think he hangs on to it far too grimly; that's why I think the stuff on induction – which doesn't depend on it – is a lot more powerful than the stuff on causation. His empiricism can be put pithily like this: 'it is impossible for us to think of any thing, which we have not antecedently felt, either by our external or internal senses' [*Enquiry* 7.4]. For example, you can't think of the taste of pineapple until you've actually tasted pineapple, or think of the colour blue until you've seen the colour blue, and so on. So when we talk about a *necessary connexion* or a *power* or a *force*, there's an idea. (And we could go into why Hume thinks these terms all signify essentially the same idea; I think he's looking for a common element, the *consequentiality* of one thing leading to another, that idea.) Where does that idea come from? On his own principles, he's got to find an impression-source for it. So he sets off trying to find an impression. And famously he finds the impression in constant conjunctions and our tendency to make inductive inferences. So when I see A followed by B again and again and again, and then I see an A, I just find myself inferring a B. Hume says that that transition of the mind, that determination to believe in B having seen an A, that is the impression of necessary connexion. This seems very odd. An impression? An impression is supposed to be something like a feeling or an impression of sense, like the impression of blue when I see blue or the impression of anger when I feel anger. (The same empiricist principle applies to internal sensations: you can't think of anger until you've felt it.) So when I feel anger, that's a feeling. But when I'm inferring a B having seen an A, it's not so clear that *that's* a *feeling*. I suspect that Hume is trying to shoehorn, as it were, the truth to fit into his theory. So he calls it 'an impression', but really, it's not an impression. It's more like *the awareness of having made an inference*, and I think that can make more sense of his theory of causation – but we can't go there now.

I've already mentioned some contributions of Don to this debate but I want to mention another. Don, in his book, drew attention to the fact that there are two definitions of *virtue* or *personal merit* in the moral *Enquiry*, just as there are two definitions of causation in both the *Treatise* and the first *Enquiry*. One of them is:

> every quality of the mind, which is *useful* or *agreeable* to the *person himself* or to others, communicates a pleasure to the spectator, engages his esteem, and is admitted under the honourable denomination of virtue or merit. [1751, 9.12, cf. 9.1]

Essentially, *virtue* or *merit* here is something that's useful or agreeable. But then the other definition is very different:

> The hypothesis which we embrace is plain. It maintains, that morality is determined by sentiment. It defines virtue to be *whatever mental action or quality gives to a spectator the pleasing sentiment of approbation*; and vice the contrary. [1751, Appendix 1.10]

What's going on here is that Hume says moral sentiments come from the sort of approbation we feel towards actions when we view them from an impartial point of view. So we see someone doing something good; maybe it doesn't benefit us, maybe it even benefits our enemy, but we think of it from an abstract point of view: 'Ah, yes, that's a good thing!' We feel this characteristic sentiment of approbation. Until you've felt that sentiment, you don't know what moral words mean; until you've got that impression, moral ideas will mean nothing to you. But Hume doesn't stop there. He doesn't just say 'that's what right and wrong is'. No; he goes on to look at all the things that we characterise as good and bad, as virtues or vices, and he systematises them – and then he says, 'Oh look! Virtually everything that we call virtue is useful or agreeable ...' But there are a few things that people call virtues that aren't like that, the monkish virtues such as celibacy, fasting, penance, mortification, self-denial, silence, solitude, etc. So what we do, is to take those from the catalogue of virtues and put them in the catalogue of vices [1751, 9.3]. They're not actually virtues, because they don't match up to this characterisation that we've found. Now Don suggested, and I think he's dead right, that what's going on with the definitions of cause is very similar. There's this characteristic inference, and you don't know what *causation* means, you don't know what *power* or *necessity* mean, until you've been in the position of inferring B from A. That gives you the inferential bit: 'Ah, I see! – that's what it is to ascribe a cause: it's to be prepared to infer one thing from another in this way.' But then Hume says: now do it *systematically*. You should ascribe causes if, and only if, crudely, there's a constant conjunction. There are lots of complications here, to do with the 'rules by which to judge of causes and effects' [*Treatise* 1.3.15], and searching for hidden causes, and various other complications – but we can't go there now.

In my view, the absolutely knock-down argument that Hume really does mean what he says when he advances this position – I mean, apart from the fact that he does actually say it – is in 'Of the immateriality of the soul' and 'Of liberty and necessity', two sections in the *Treatise* [1.4.5 and 2.3.1 respectively]. Basically, in both cases what he's aiming to do is to say that causation, the same kind of causation that applies to billiard balls, applies just as much to the actions of human beings. So in the first case, in 'Of the immateriality of the soul', he's attacking people who say that the motion of matter cannot possibly cause thought because it's just so different from thought: there's no way thought can arise from *that*. And lots of people, including Locke and Clarke, used this for theological purposes, including the Cosmological Argument – they wanted to prove that there must be a thinking being responsible for all this, because if you didn't have thinking to start with, it could never have come about from pure matter. In response to this, Hume says, 'Many people think this is a strong argument. But actually it's ever so easy to refute. Just think about what we know about cause and effect. Cause and effect is all about constant conjunction, and anything can be constantly conjoined with anything: in particular, motion can be constantly conjoined with thought. Oh – and it is! So 'motion may be, and actually is, the cause of thought and perception' [*Treatise* 1.4.5.30]. That's how he argues, very explicitly, in the last few paragraphs of section 1.4.5 of the *Treatise*. In 'Of liberty and necessity', he's got a different target, namely, people who think that the kind of causation that applies to human beings is completely different from the kind of causation that applies to billiard balls. Again, a very quick answer: Hume just says, 'Well, you know those two definitions of "cause" – they capture everything we can understand by a cause. And it all comes down to constant conjunction and inference. So now let's look at the moral world, human behaviour. Oh, look! There's constant conjunction, and there's inference. It's the same causation, exactly the same. And anyone who thinks that there's some extra causation in physical things: they don't know what they're talking about! They haven't even got an idea of what it is that they're looking for.' Given the way the texts go, these interpretative arguments seem to me to be pretty much knock-down – and I think Don and I are agreed on that aren't we?

Q: When I used to teach statistics to third-year students, I used to tell them that statistical constant conjunction was equivalent to a statistical correlation just to make a historical connection – I never actually checked whether that was right or wrong with a philosopher ... But I think I used to say that necessary connection was a kind of mathematical process of deduction, so I was clearly wrong about that!

PM: Hume does recognise a conceptual necessity as well as causal necessity – but in simplifying, I was leaving that out. He does want to insist that there's only one kind of *causal* necessity, whereas his opponents, like Clarke, wanted to say there's a difference between *physical* and *moral* necessity. One of the first things that Hume does when he's given his two definitions is that he says here's a corollary: there is no distinction between physical and moral necessity. But he leaves conceptual necessity intact. One can debate all sort of things about that too.

Q: So I wasn't completely wrong?

PM: No! [Laughter]

SM: Well, thank you very much. We'll hope to continue discussion over some drinks next door and I do invite you to join us. I'm not going to adjudicate between reasoning and ratiocination [laughter] but we have most certainly seen a wonderful example of philosophical thinking in action. Thanks very much, it's been a terrific dialogue. [Applause]

DG: Peter and I both thank the Institute for making this possible.

PM: Very much so! I have to say, it's been wonderful, it really has, this week and on an earlier occasion too, debating with Don about all this for hours on end.

DG: We've been here for several days together... You might be able to tell... [Laughter]

PM: It's been a wonderful opportunity.

DG: Yes, give us another week and we'll solve everything!

Bibliography

Beauchamp, T. L. and Mappes, T. J. 1975. 'Is Hume Really a Sceptic about Induction?', *American Philosophical Quarterly* 12, pp. 119-129.

Beattie. J. 1770. *An Essay on the Nature and Immutability of Truth.* London: Edward and Charles Dilly.

Beebee, H. 2006. *Hume on Causation.* London and New York: Routledge.

Blackburn, S. 1993. *Essays in Quasi-Realism.* New York: Oxford University Press.

Coventry, A. 2006. *Hume's Theory of Causation: A Quasi-Realist Interpretation.* London: Continuum.

Flew, A. 1961. *Hume's Philosophy of Belief.* London: Routledge and Kegan Paul.

Garrett, D. 1997. *Cognition and Commitment in Hume's Philosophy.* New York: Oxford University Press.

Garrett, D. 1998. 'Ideas, Reason, and Skepticism: Replies to my Critics', *Hume Studies* 24, pp. 171-194.

Hartley, D. 1749. *Observations on Man, His Frame, His Duty, and His Expectations.* Bath and London: Printed by S. Richardson; for James Leake and Wm. Frederick.

Hume, D. 1739-40 [2007]. *A Treatise of Human Nature.* Ed. D. F. Norton, M. J. Norton. Oxford: Clarendon Press.

Hume, David. 1745. *A Letter from a Gentleman to his Friend in Edinburgh.* Edinburgh: [s.n.].

Hume, D. 1748 [2007]. *An Enquiry concerning Human Understanding.* Ed. P. J. R. Millican. Oxford: Oxford University Press.

Hume, D. 1751 [1998]. *An Enquiry concerning the Principles of Morals.* Ed. T. L. Beauchamp. Oxford: Clarendon Press.

Hume, D. 1757 [2007]. *A Dissertation on the Passions and The Natural History of Religion.* Ed. T. L. Beauchamp. Oxford: Clarendon Press.

Hume, D. 1779 [1947]. *Dialogues concerning Natural Religion*. Ed. N. Kemp Smith, 2nd ed. London: T. Nelson.

Hutcheson, F. 1742. *An Essay on the Nature and Conduct of the Passions and Affections. With Illustrations on the Moral Sense*, 3rd ed. London: A. Ward.

Hutcheson, F. 1744 [2006]. *Synopsis of Metaphysics*, in F. Hutcheson, *Logic, Metaphysics, and the Natural Sociability of Mankind*. Ed. J. Moore and M. Silverthorne. Tr. M. Silverthorne. Indianapolis: Liberty Fund.

Hutcheson, F. 1747 [2007]. *A Short Introduction to Moral Philosophy*. Ed. L. Turco. Tr. anonymously from *Philosophiae Moralis Institutio Compendiaria*, 2nd ed. Indianapolis: Liberty Fund.

Locke, J. 1690 [1975]. *An Essay concerning Human Understanding*. Ed. P. H. Nidditch. Oxford: Oxford University Press.

Millican, P. J. R. 1995. 'Hume's Argument Concerning Induction: Structure and Interpretation', in *David Hume: Critical Assessments*. Ed. S. Tweyman. London and New York: Routledge, pp. 91-144.

Millican, P. J. R. 1998. 'Hume on Reason and Induction: Epistemology or Cognitive Science?', *Hume Studies* 24, pp. 141-159.

Millican, P. J. R. 2002. 'Hume's Sceptical Doubts Concerning Induction', in *Reading Hume on Human Understanding*. Ed. P. J. R. Millican. Oxford: Clarendon Press, pp. 107-173.

Millican, P. J. R. 2007. 'Against the New Hume', in *The New Hume Debate*. Ed. R. Read, K. Richman, rev. ed. London and New York: Routledge, pp. 211-252.

Millican, P. J. R. 2009. 'Hume, Causal Realism, and Causal Science', *Mind* 118, pp. 647–712.

Price, R. 1758. *A Review of the Principal Questions and Difficulties in Morals*. London: Millar.

Stove, D. C. 1973. *Probability and Hume's Inductive Scepticism*. Oxford: Clarendon Press.

Strawson, G. 1989. *The Secret Connexion: Causation, Realism, and David Hume.* Oxford: Oxford University Press.

Wright, J. P. 1983. *The Sceptical Realism of David Hume.* Manchester: Manchester University Press.